JIM BRICKMAN

by heart

PIA... ...S

Album Graphic Design by Barbara Vick
Cover Photography by Cristiana Ceppas

Project Manager: Jeannette DeLisa
Art Layout: Odalis Soto

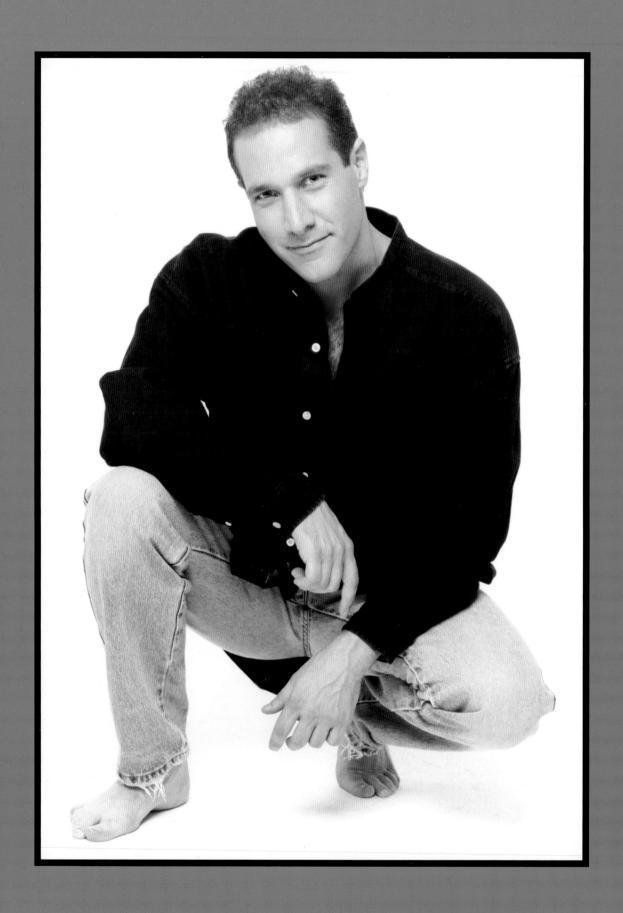

JIM BRICKMAN

CONTENTS

ANGEL EYES

Composed by
JIM BRICKMAN

Brightly

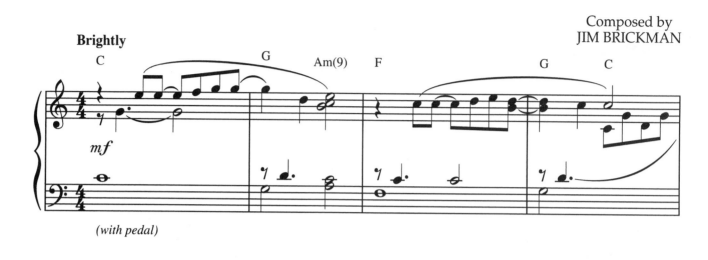

(with pedal)

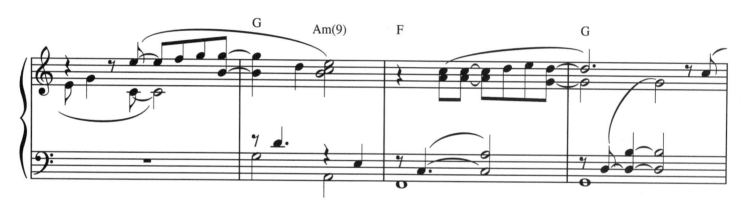

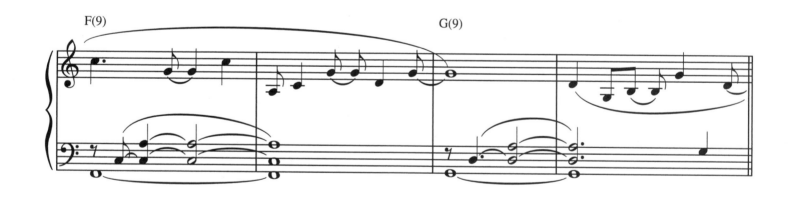

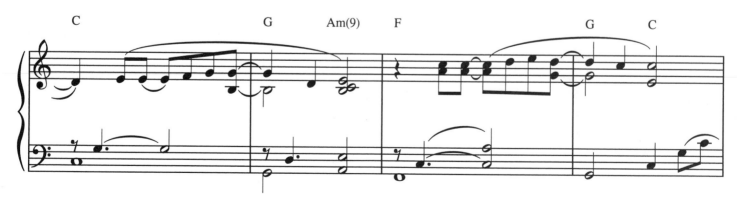

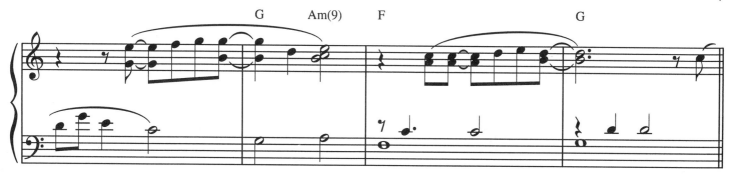

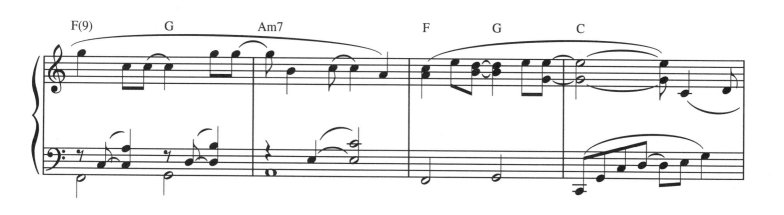

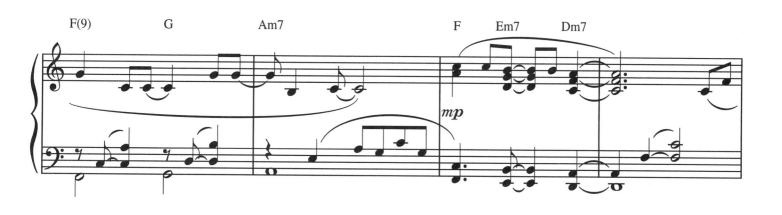

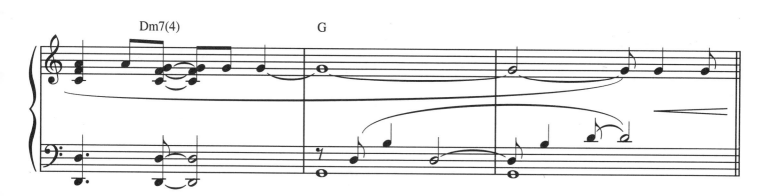

8

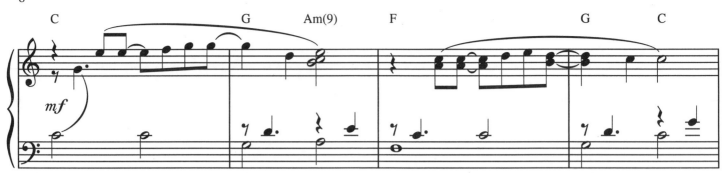

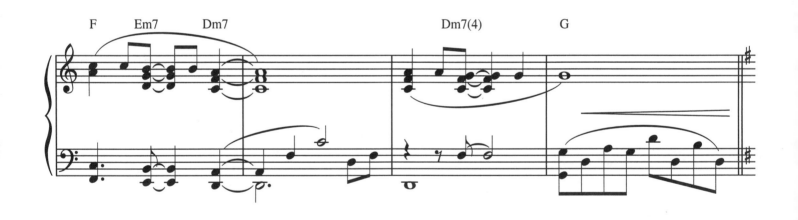

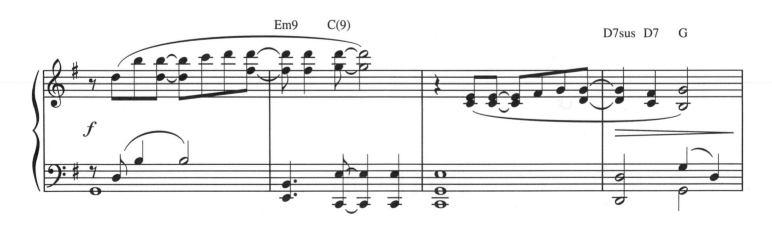

If You Believe

Composed by
JIM BRICKMAN

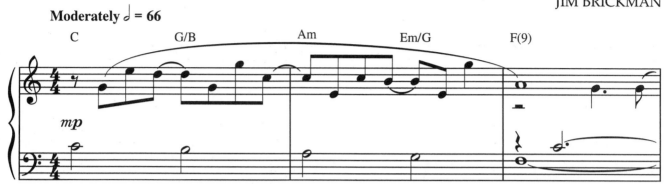

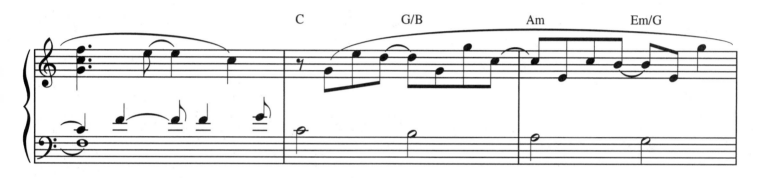

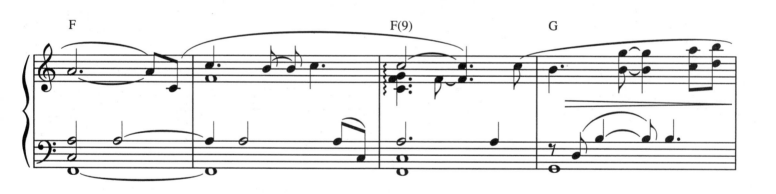

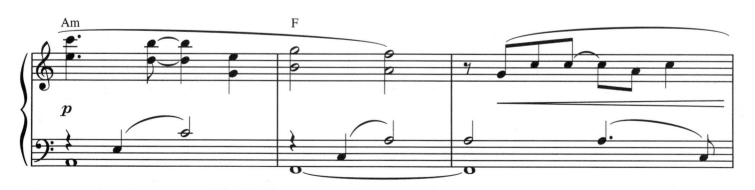

If You Believe - 5 - 1
PF9542

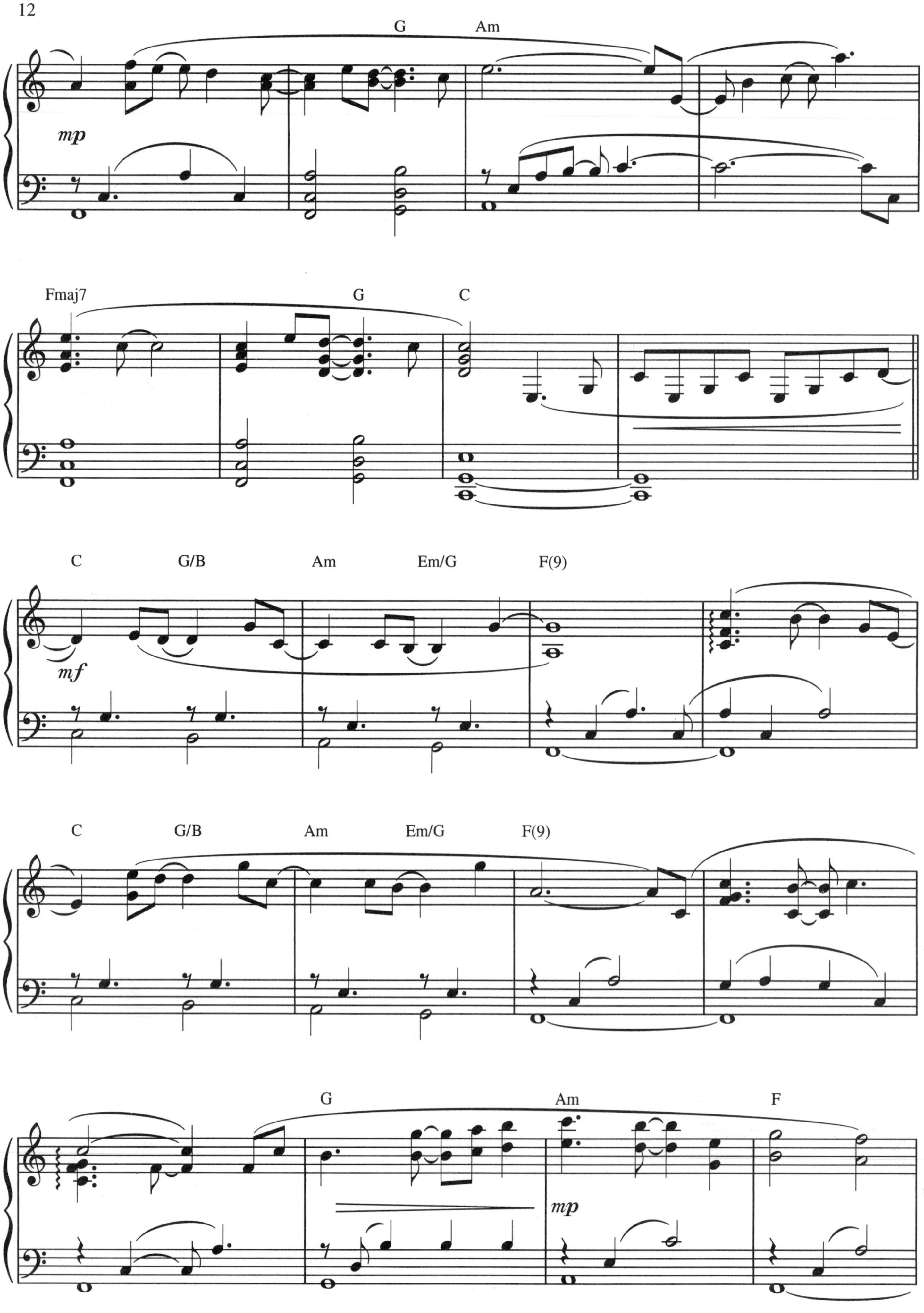
G
Am
mp
Fmaj7
G
C
C
G/B
Am
Em/G
F(9)
mf
C
G/B
Am
Em/G
F(9)
G
Am
F
mp

14

LITTLE STAR

Composed by
JIM BRICKMAN

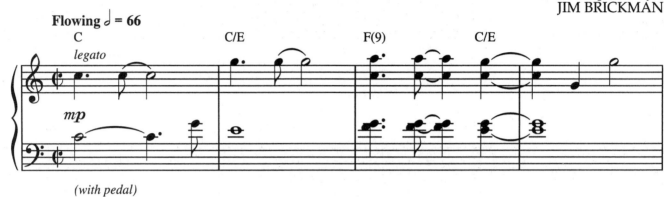

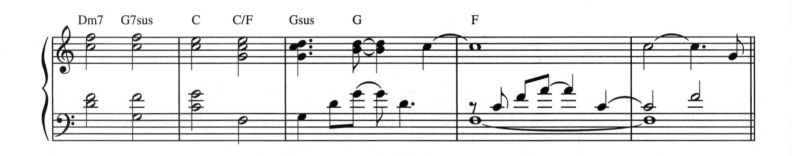

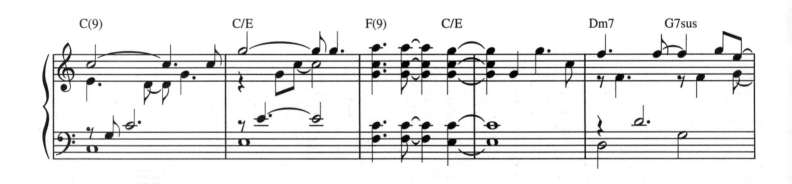

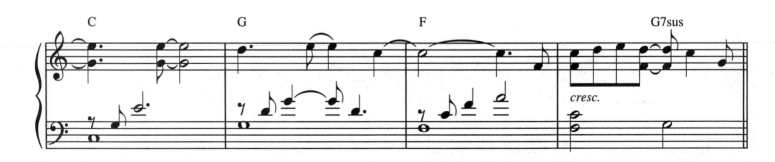

Little Star - 6 - 1
PF9542

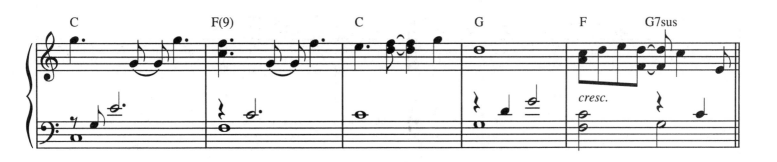

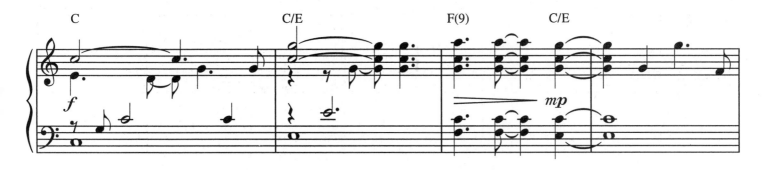

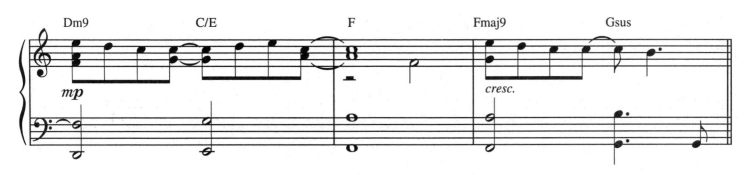

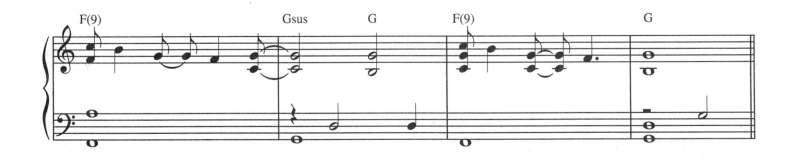

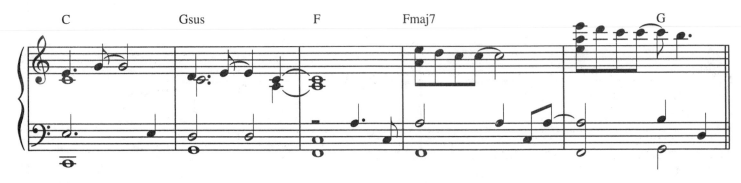

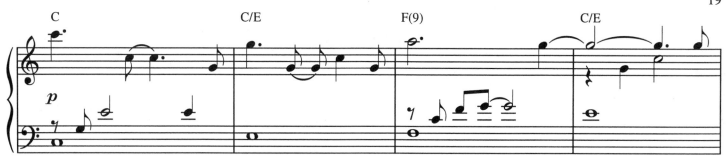

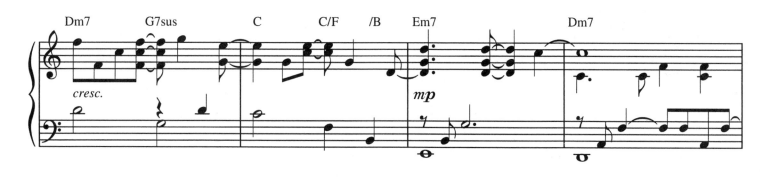

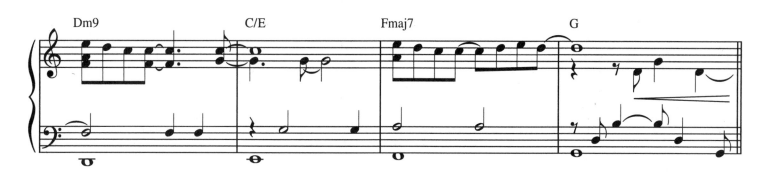

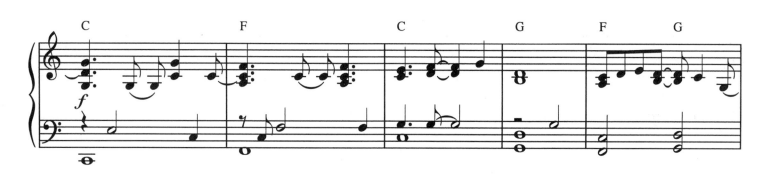

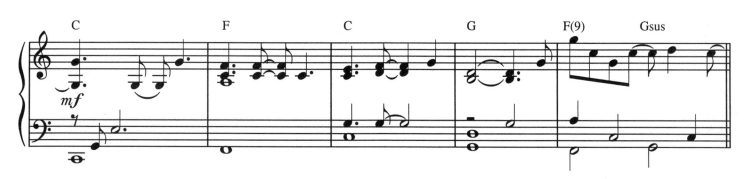

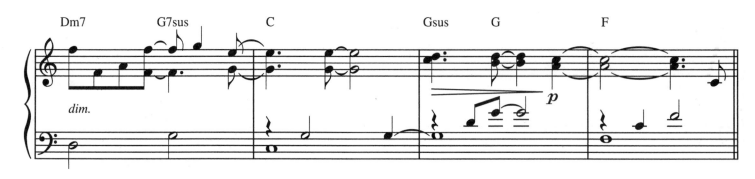

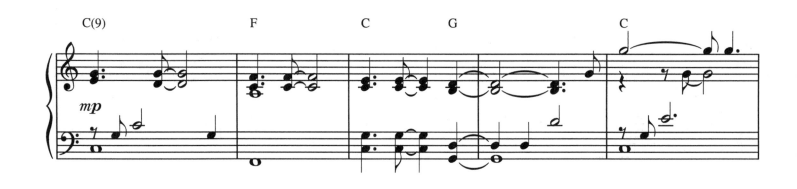

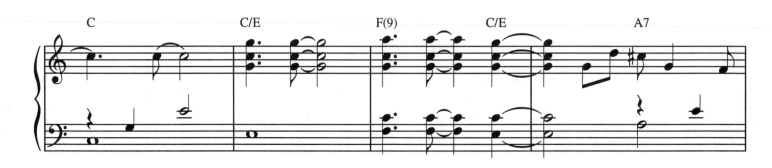

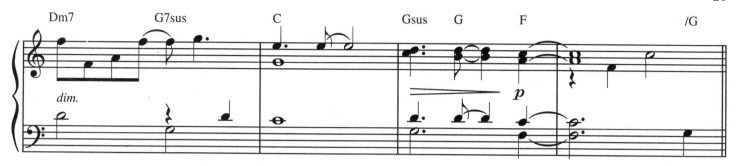

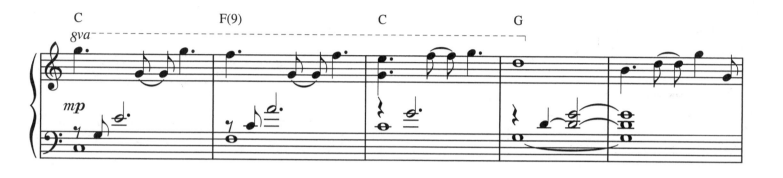

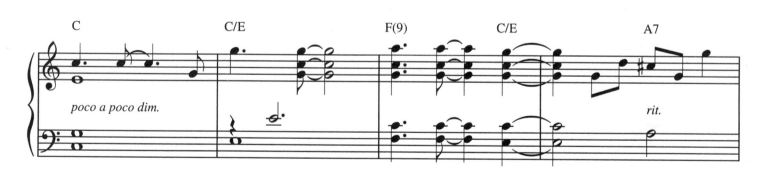

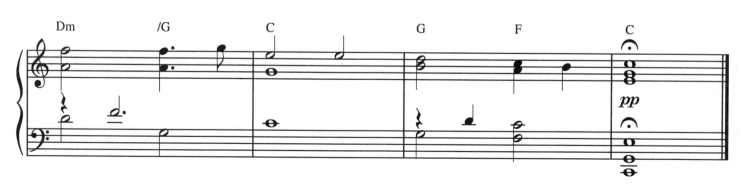

All I Ever Wanted

Composed by
JIM BRICKMAN

LAKE ERIE RAINFALL

Composed by
JIM BRICKMAN

Flowing ♩ = 63

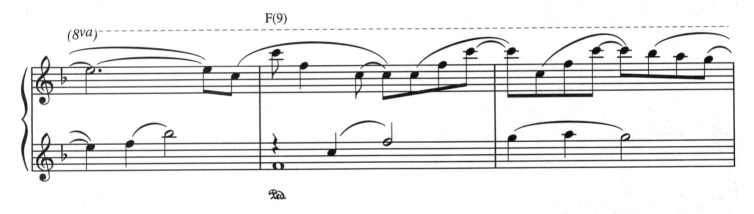

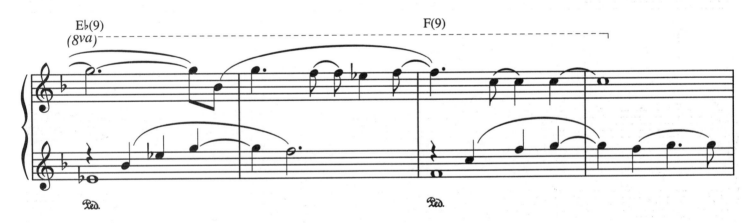

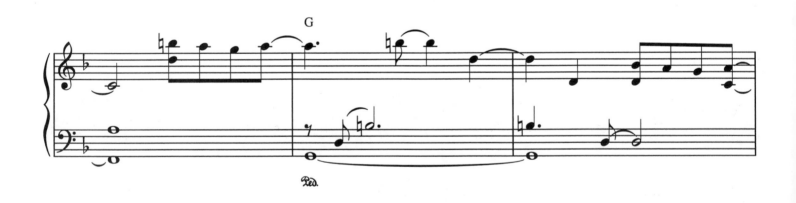

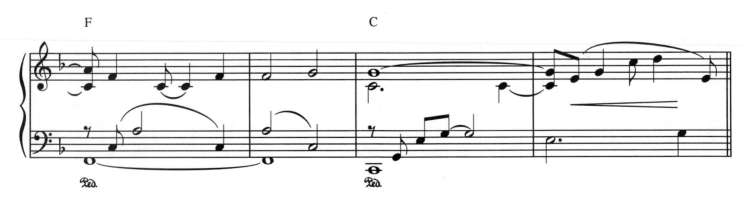

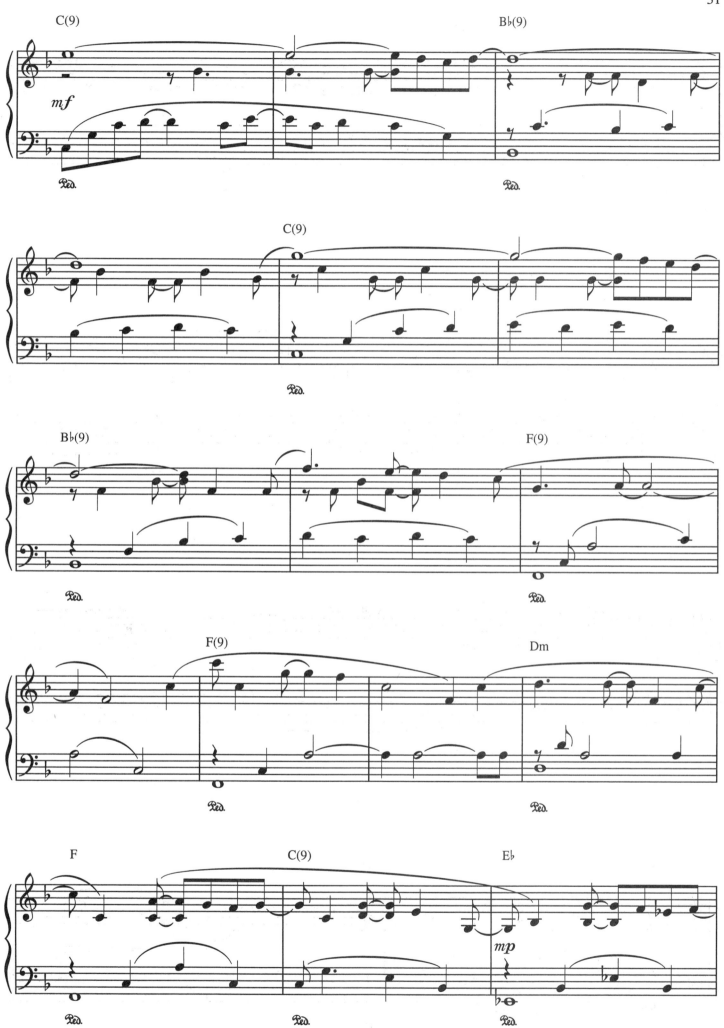

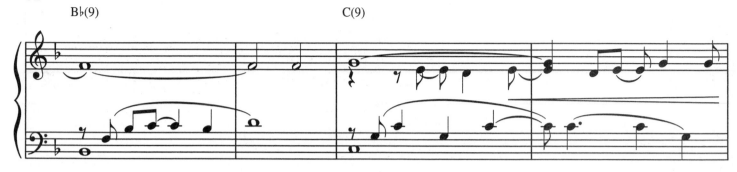

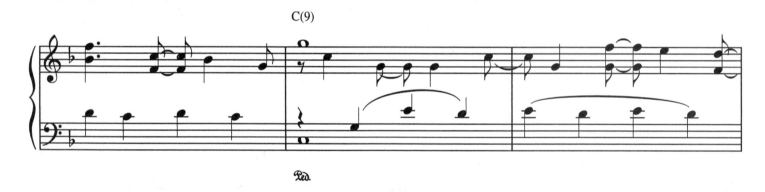

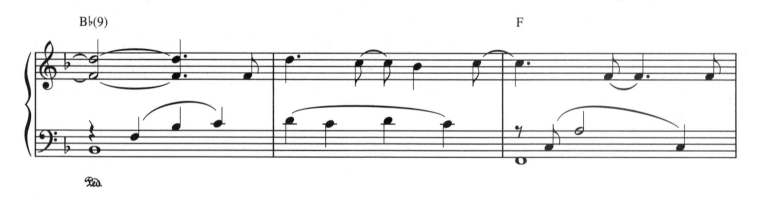

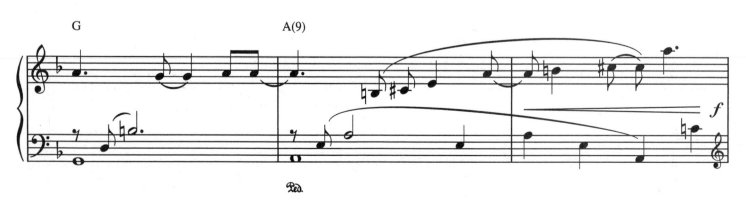

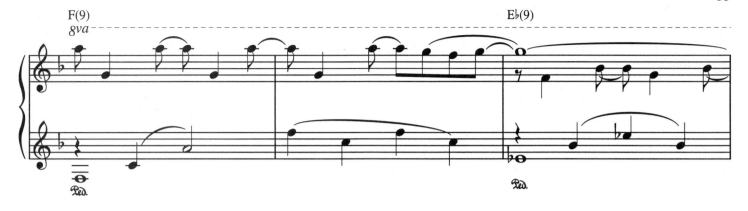

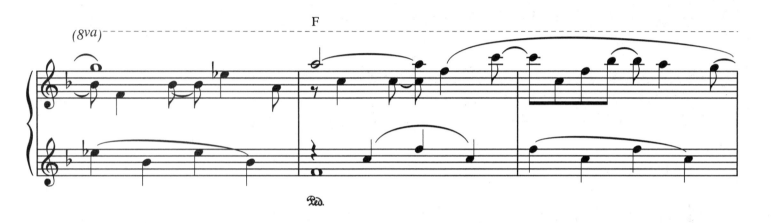

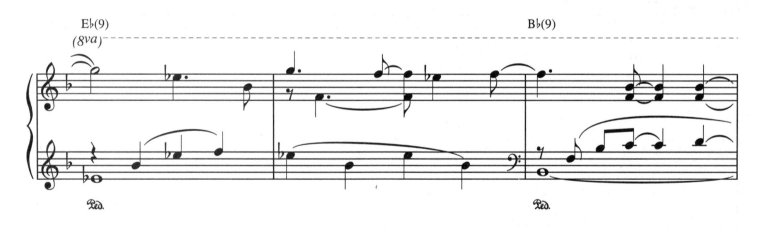

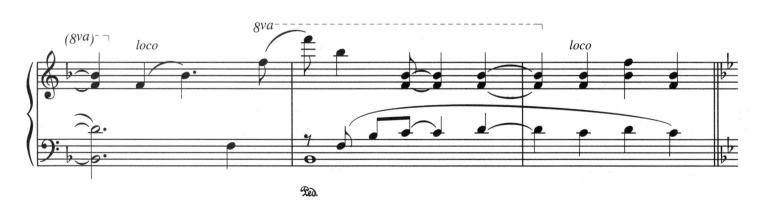

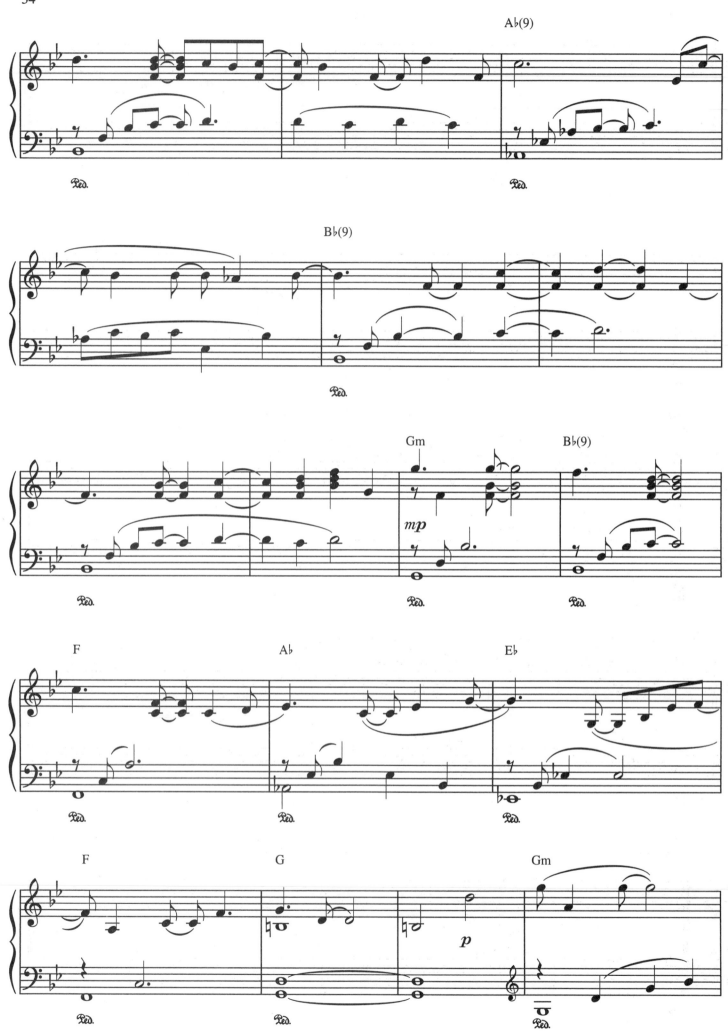

SUDDEN INSPIRATION

Composed by
JIM BRICKMAN

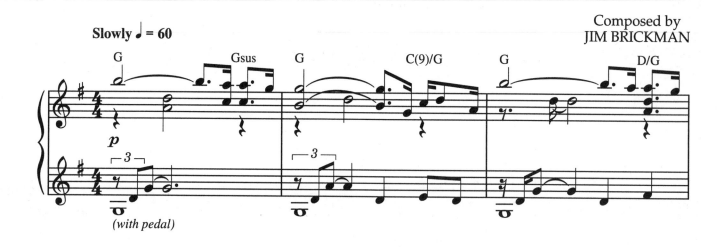

Sudden Inspiration - 4 - 1
PF9542

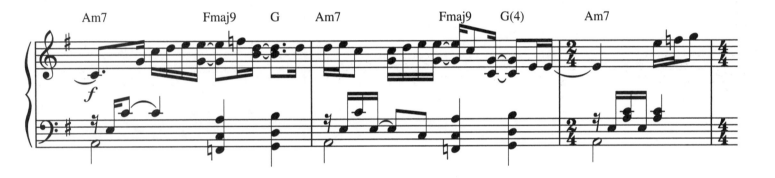

Nothing Left To Say

Composed by
JIM BRICKMAN

Slowly, with freedom

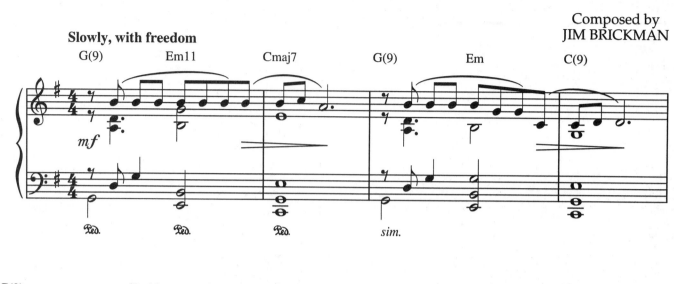

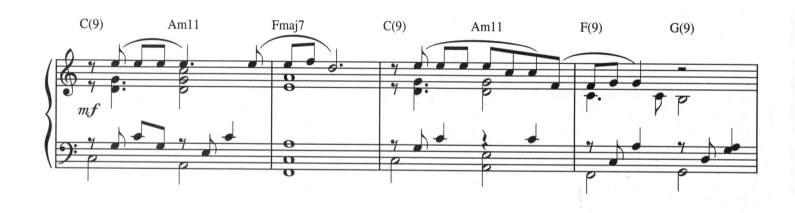

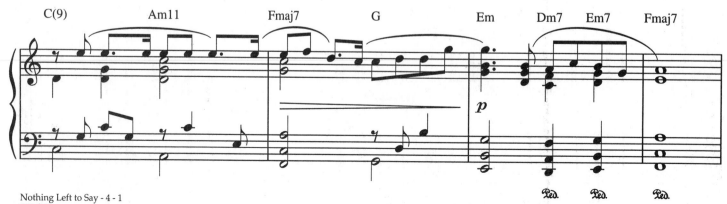

Nothing Left to Say - 4 - 1
PF9542

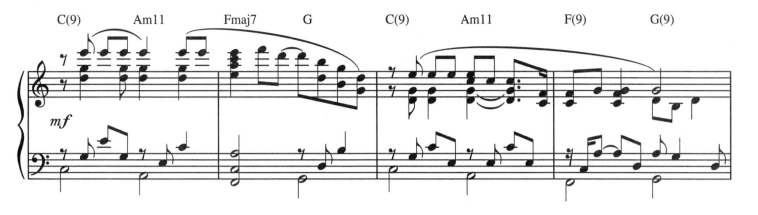

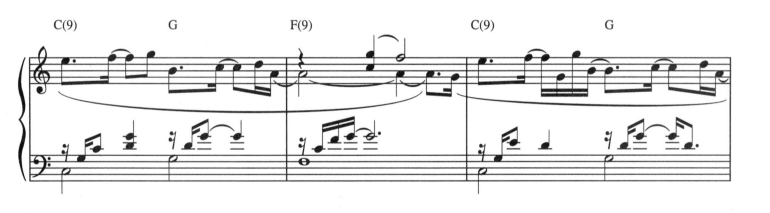

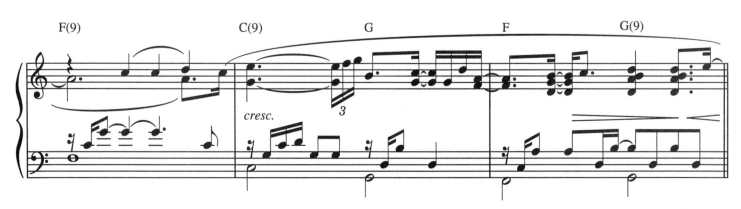

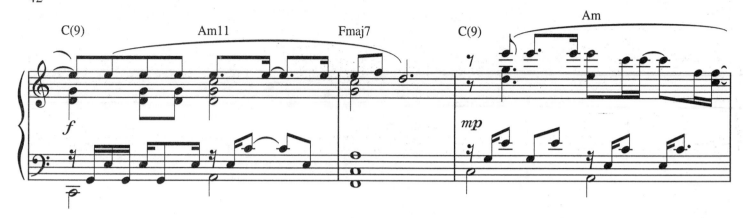

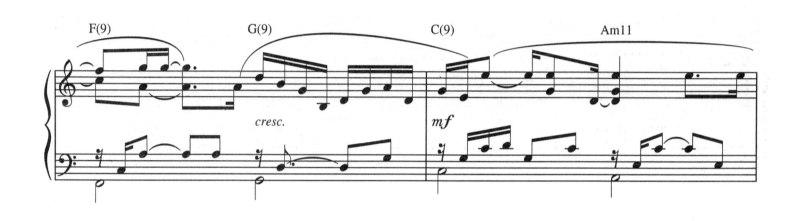

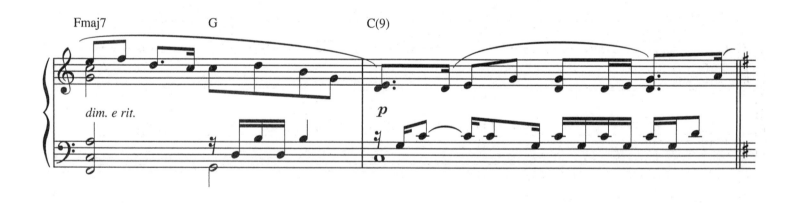

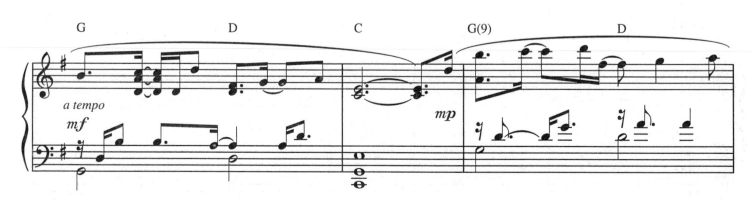

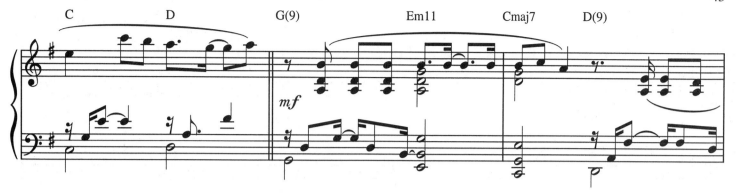

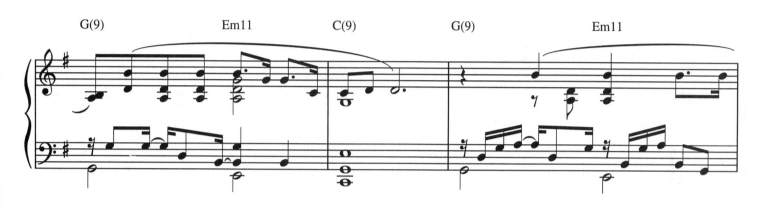

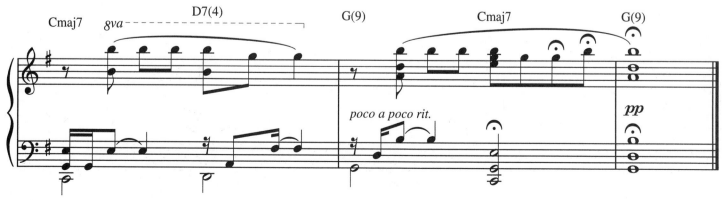

WHERE ARE YOU NOW?

Composed by
JIM BRICKMAN

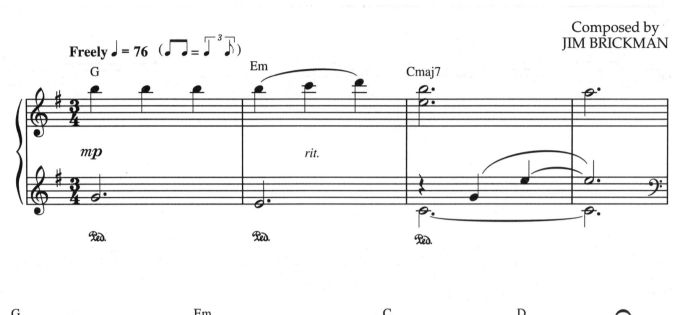

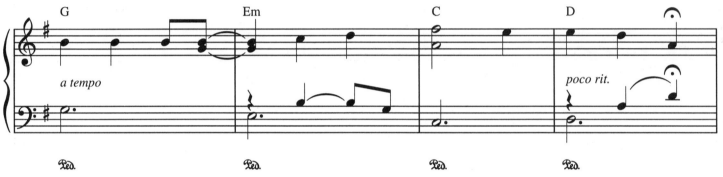

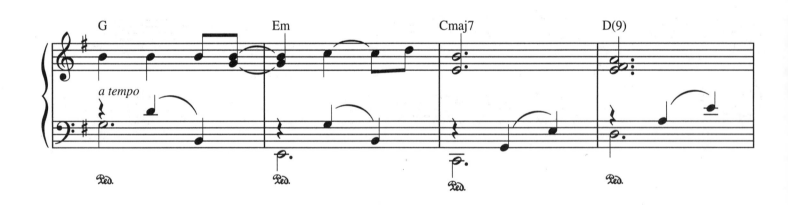

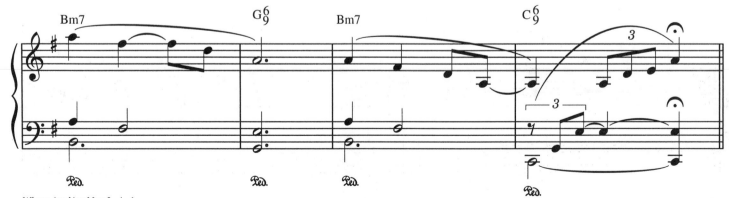

Where Are You Now? - 4 - 1
PF9542

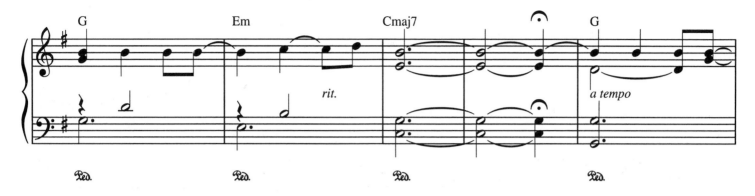

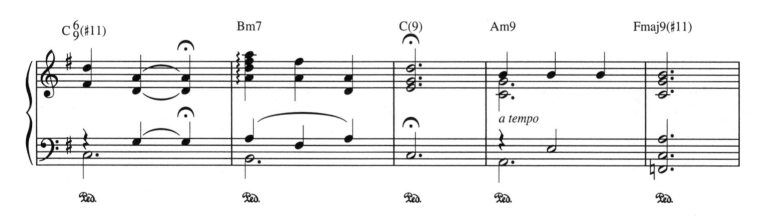

By Heart

Composed by
JIM BRICKMAN and
HOLLYE LEVEN

Slowly ♩ = 63   *Verse:*

1. Hold me close,__ ba - by, please.__
2. When you go,__ I'll stop__ the clock.__

Tell me an - y-thing but that you're gon - na leave.__
I won't ev - er let this mo - ment stop.__

As I kiss__ this fall - en tear,__ I
Time is steal - in' you__ from me,__ but it can

By Heart - 4 - 1
PF9542

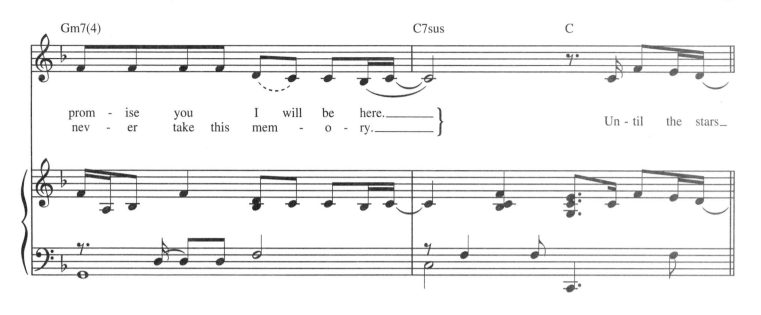

prom - ise you I will be here._____
nev - er take this mem - o - ry._____ }

Un - til the stars_

℅ *Chorus:*

___ fall from the sky, un - til I find____ a rea - son why,_ and, dar-ling,

as the___ years___ go___ by,_____ un - til there's no__

In A Lover's Eyes

Composed by
JIM BRICKMAN and
BROCK WALSH

Moderately ♩ = 50

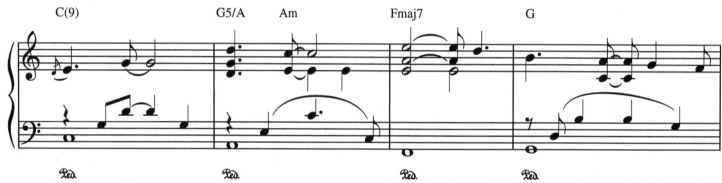

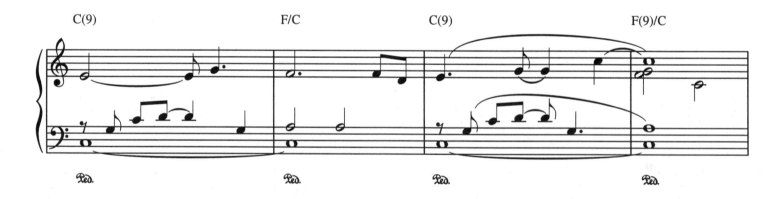

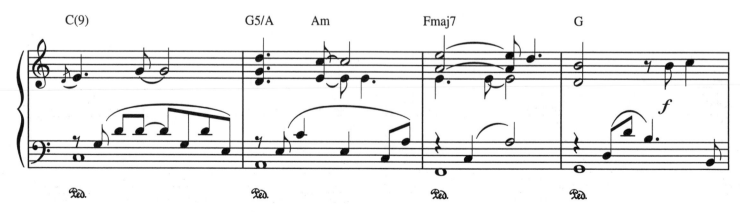

In a Lover's Eyes - 5 - 1
PF9542

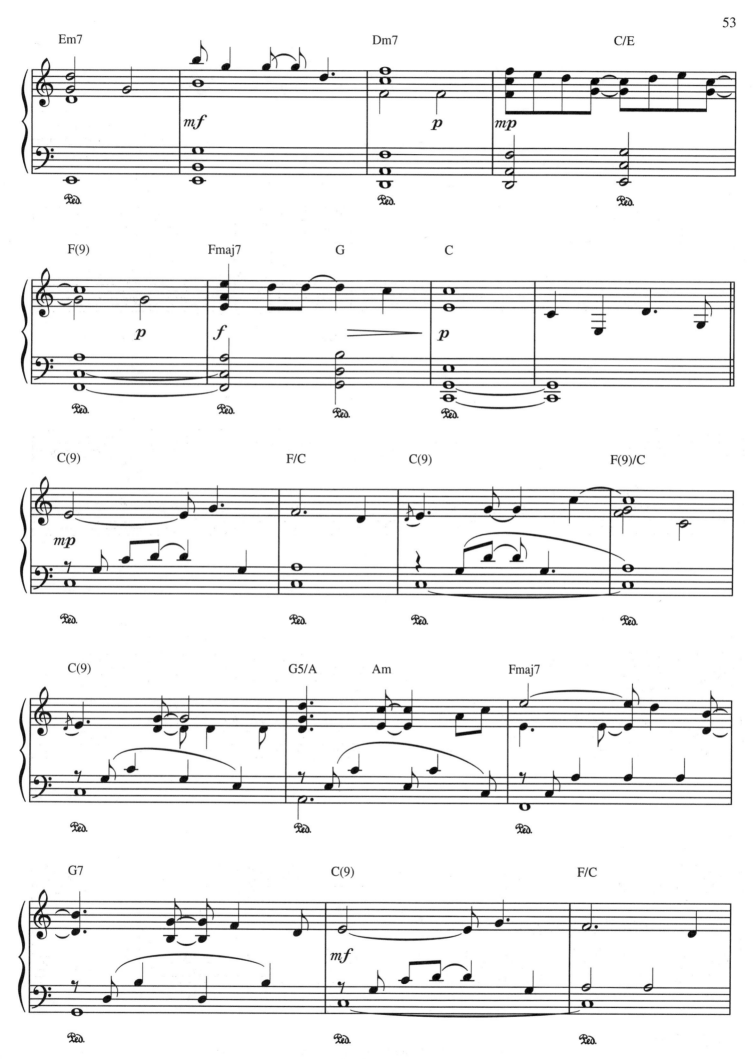

LOOKING BACK

Composed by
JIM BRICKMAN

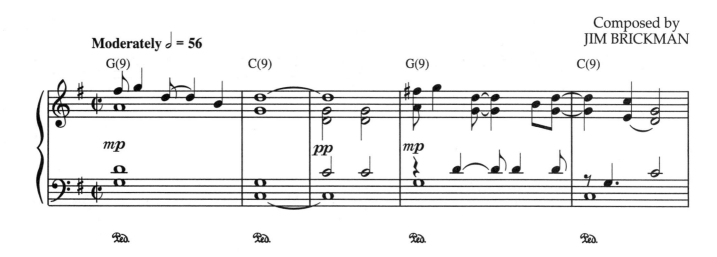

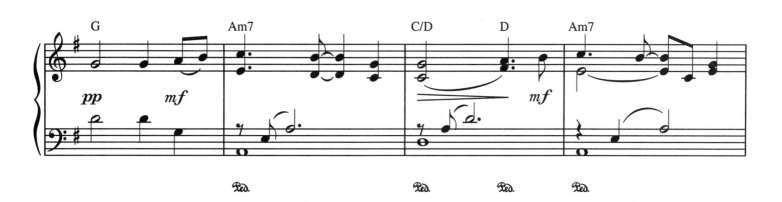

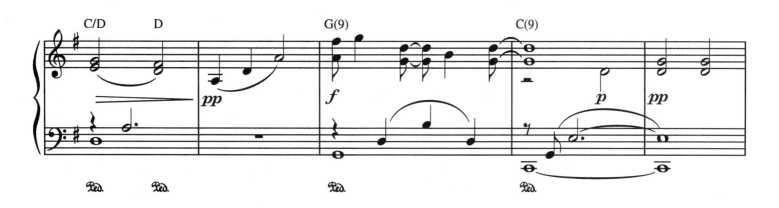

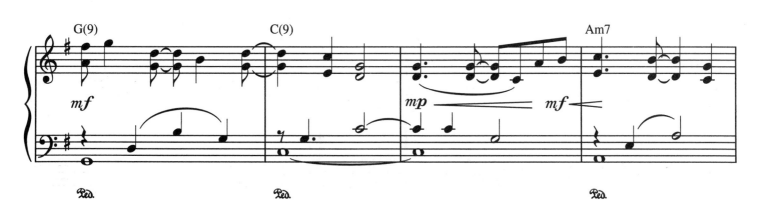

Looking Back - 5 - 1
PF9542

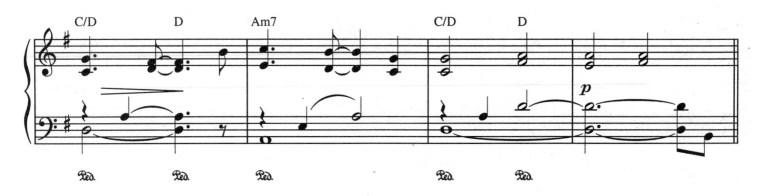

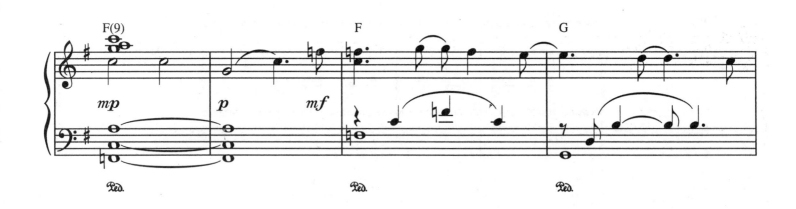

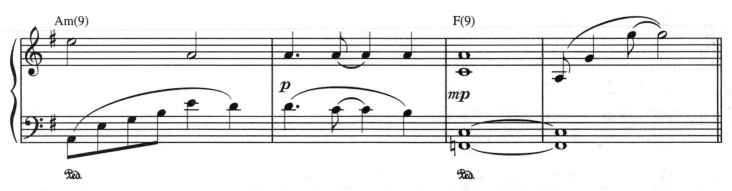

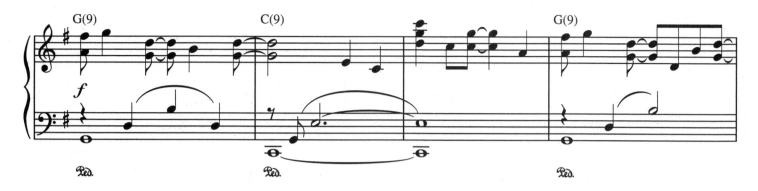

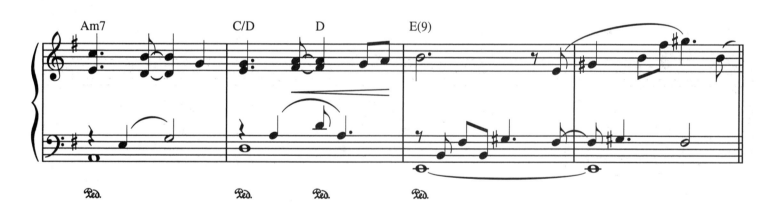

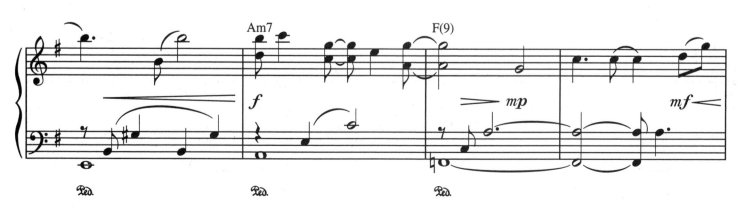

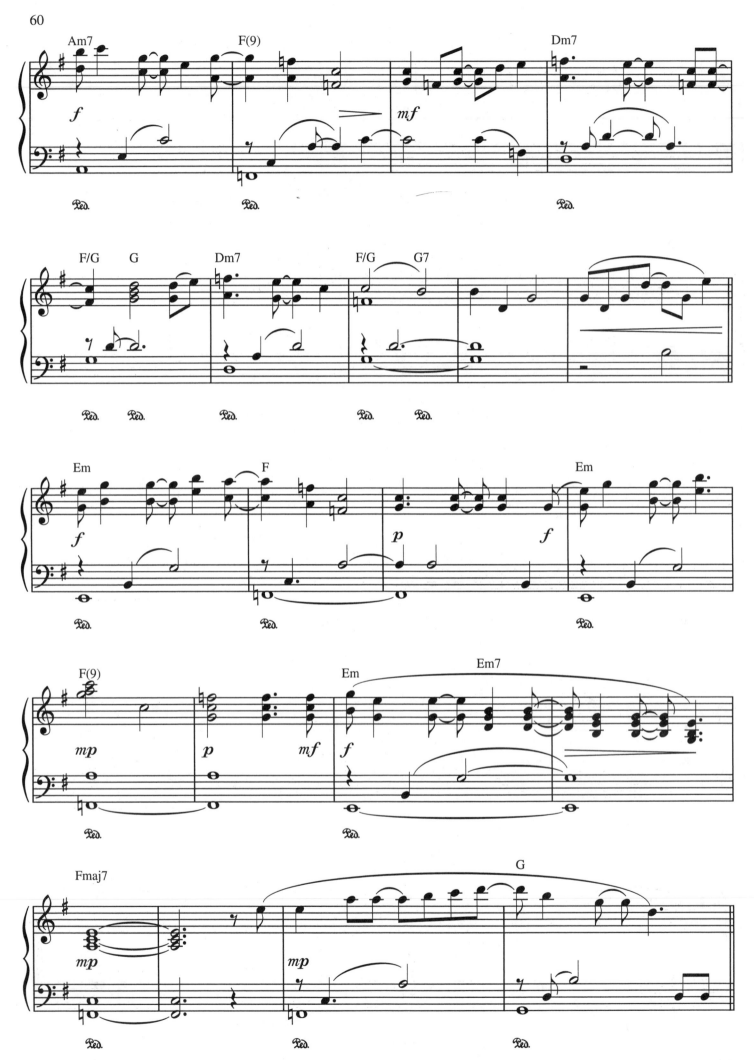

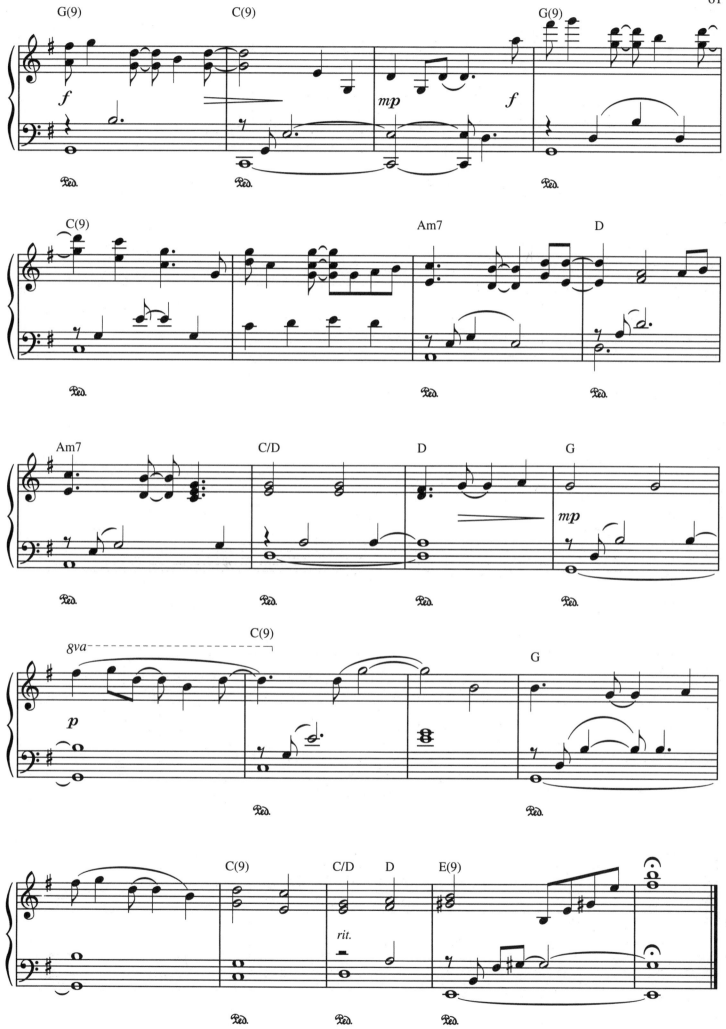

On The Edge

Composed by
JIM BRICKMAN

On the Edge - 7 - 1
PF9542

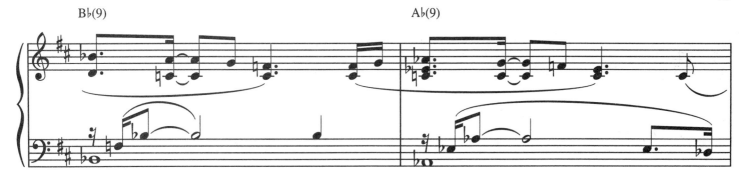

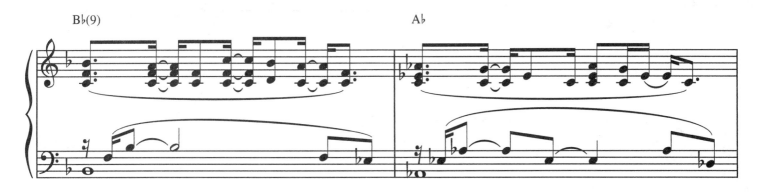

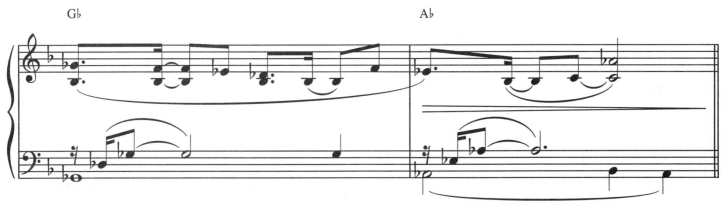

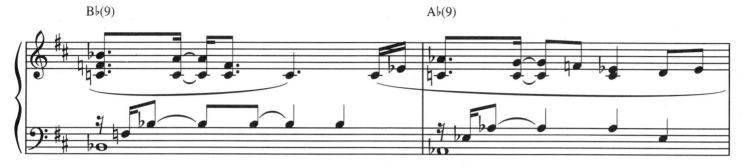

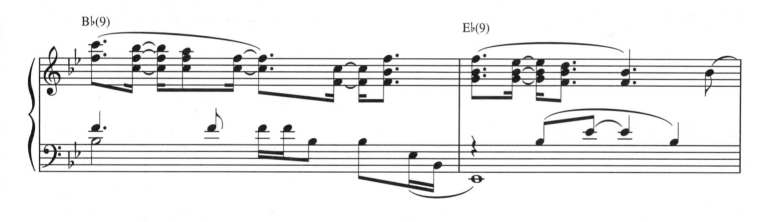

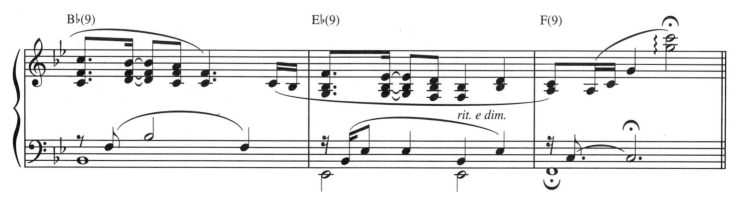

JIM BRICKMAN

by heart

"I follow my heart. It's as simple as that."

Simplicity is at the heart of *By Heart*, the second solo album by pianist Jim Brickman. That's "solo" as in alone. Just two hands and 88 keys.

And of course, a few surprises, including sublime cameos from a vibraphone, a cello and—on the closing cut, the upbeat "By Heart"—a vocalist. One thing hasn't changed: every lilting tune melts your heart and puts a smile on your face.

As a music conservatory black sheep more interested in pop than Pachelbel, Brickman has always maintained his belief in the power of a simple melody. Undaunted, he followed his heart and began paving the way for solo recordings with the inviting and unforgettable themes of his '94 debut album. *No Words* lived up to its name. Call it truth in advertising (after all, Brickman first honed his craft as a prolific jingle composer for 7-Up, AT&T, Sony, McDonalds, etc.), because the album broke the mold with friendly, hummable pop songs presented on solo piano. No band, no vocals, no lofty pretentions.

In the same way, *By Heart* rings true. Note the immediacy of the one-take wonder, "On The Edge," a duet with cello. Hear the powerfully direct melodies of "If You Believe" and the child-like playfulness of "Little Star," Jim's sparkling take on "Twinkle, Twinkle" that concludes each concert.

Brickman is most pleased—and *grateful*—that his informal concerts have allowed him to communicate with listeners firsthand. "People can really connect with the music because it's heartfelt and real," says the warmly personable musician who shares personal stories along with his emotional tunes. "The world is such a noisy place that this is a refreshing change; the simplicity of the whole thing is attractive. I want people to enjoy themselves, to get to know me, to feel a connection to the music, and not take everything so seriously."

Brickman's back-to-basics Tin Pan Alley sensibilities are rooted in the basics of the instrument. He's so no-nonsense that he remains staunchly loyal to the same beat-up Yamaha upright that he's played since he was 10.

Yet everything has changed since the '94 release of his dynamic debut, *No Words*. U.S. radio launched into orbit the starry single "Rocket to the Moon," making history as it became the very first solo instrumental song *ever* to score on the pop charts. Record sales jumped and new fans insisted Brickman embark on his first national concert tour.

International enthusiasm lured the Midwest native to the Far East, where magazines were far from wordless about Brickman's new pop idol status there. Brickman has accepted foreign invitations to return to Asia this year for an encore tour.

Brickman admits that he's always been "a break-the-rules kind of guy." At the Cleveland Institute of Music, the classical composition and performance student was charting his own course (solo, of course), applying his classical studies toward the mainstream. "That's what came naturally to me," he says. "Pop songwriting."

While residing in the campus dormitory, the 19-year-old committed musical sacrilege by launching his professional career as a commercial jingle writer. After composing samples and sending demos to top New York ad agencies, Brickman soon won assignments for such clients as Jim Henson and Henson Associates, writing and producing music for the Muppets and Children's Television Workshop.

Moving to L.A., he founded his own production company, The Brickman Arrangement, to create music for such clients as G.E., The Gap, Sprint, Isuzu, Kellogg's, and Disney TV movies and cartoons. An award-winning composer and performer, Brickman's work has been recognized at the Houston International Film Festival and London's International Advertising Awards, as well as the Clios, Tellys and Addy Awards.

Jim's continuing quest is for dramatic hooks and melodies that people can't help but immediately grasp and appreciate on an emotional level.

"I think of my music as a blank book. With it, listeners can take away anything they want to take away. They can sing to it, read to it, use it for romance, wake up to it on a Sunday morning.... The great thing about instrumental music is that it's not telling you how to feel. With lyrics, you're stuck with a concrete idea, but this can mean different things to you at different times of day. The right ebb and flow of sounds—unspoken emotions—can be extremely powerful because they're open to interpretation."

Have a heart-to-heart with *By Heart*.

OTHER WINDHAM HILL RELEASES BY OR FEATURING

JIM BRICKMAN

INCLUDE:

NO WORDS • PIANO SAMPLER 2 • A WINTER SOLSTICE V
WINDHAM HILL SAMPLER 1996

JIM BRICKMAN would like to invite you to be on his Mailing List to receive information about concert schedules, merchandise and upcoming releases. Please fill out the coupon below and mail to:

JIM BRICKMAN
c/o EDGE MANAGEMENT
11288 VENTURA BLVD. SUITE 606
STUDIO CITY, CA 91604

(818) 508-8400 **phone**
(818) 508-8444 **fax**

or

E-Mail us at BrickPiano@AOL.com.
Also, please visit our current Internet Site on the Worldwide Web at WINDHAM.com.

Cut Along Here ✄

NAME _____

ADDRESS _____

CITY _____ **STATE** _____ **ZIP** _____

SEX: M___ F___   **E - Mail** _____